THE ROAD OF BEING

Poetry

Germain Droogenbroodt

THE ROAD OF BEING

Poetry

Germain Droogenbroodt

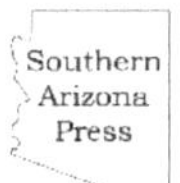

Southern Arizona Press
Sierra Vista, Arizona

The Road of Being

By Germain Droogenbroodt

First Edition

Author: Germain Droogenbroodt
Translated by Germain Droogenbroodt and Stanley H. Barkan
Cover and Interior Illustrations: Satish Gupta
Editor: Paul Gilliland
Formatting: Southern Arizona Press

Published by Southern Arizona Press
Sierra Vista, Arizona 85635
www.SouthernArizonaPress.com

ISBN: 978-1-960038-35-7

Poetry

INTRODUCTION

WAITING FOR BETTER TIMES

The Road of Being, Germain Droogenbroodt's latest poetry book, represents a new inflection in his already long career, with sixteen poetry collections published, several of them published in thirty countries. Although in the three parts that make up the set we will find diverse thematic approaches and interests, they all converge in that backbone that constitutes a concise and suggestive style that makes Germain Droogenbroodt's poetry unmistakable.

The first block with which the book opens, refers to the mostly meditative part of his previous poetry, where the light of dawn, the flight of the birds detached from the earthly, the opening of the flowers, the miraculous beating of the heart . . . lead to a serene and peaceful panorama. And like that same dawn, territory of the unpredictable, of what is always to come, so the poet, "with words / that only silence / knows how to express," also does not know in advance the verses that will appear. To create is to obtain that vision, that luminosity, that illumination, which poetry offers and which is not only "a shelter for the word." A vision, with our eyes closed and turned inward, that allows us to see with total lucidity the external reality. The poem then becomes that bridge that reintegrates the inner with the outer, the poet, the human being, with nature.

In *Witnesses of a Time*, not by chance the central part of the book, at the antipodes of all the above, we look at the crude reality in which we live: human alienation (entertainment) and control (surveillance by digital devices) in this technocratic world, in which also vanity and hatred so thriving in social networks represent the agony of discursive communication, of argumentation or even of personal thought itself: others (a robot, a chip) end up thinking for us. And with this agony, democracy is wounded and looks into the abyss of totalitarian horizons.

Depersonalization, environmental deterioration, anxiety, and mental illness . . . lead us to ask ourselves "But is life / that is no longer dignified / still life?"

In *Without Return*, the third and last part of the collection, we find poems that allude to the passage of time and our futile resistance to stop it, to the ephemeral and the changing, to our vulnerability and the ups and downs of life, to its fleetingness, to the non-return of what has already been lived, except in memory; to the autumn of man and his unavoidable path towards death. A death that, beyond the inequalities in which we live, definitely makes us all equal. Death sometimes also painful, and in the most absolute loneliness, as in the case of those killed by covid in the hospital: "None knocking at the door / nobody you expect, / no one, except death."

The book closes with several poems about the invasion and war in Ukraine: all the horror of extreme violence and destruction in the image of a rope around the neck of the dove of peace, our most human helplessness, our immense fragility.

After reading, it seems evident that the poet shows us by contrast how is the reality in which we live today and how it should be for it to be a dignified life. Thus, while man's search should lead him to the light (as expressed in one of the opening poems of the book), the reality we are witnessing leads us, through the subway tunnels of the technocratic mole, to the most fearsome darkness. Although if there is one thing Germain Droogenbroodt does not lose, as poets have never lost, it is hope: just as "that after the rain, / the sun will shine." Man continues to trust and hope—like the winter birds—for the arrival of "better times." That is his last verse in the book, his augured horizon, the greatest longing in these rather dark times. Such is, or should be, *The Road of Being*.

–Rafael Carcelén

Contents

The Goal 12
Meditation 13
The Light 14
Cinders 15
Search 16
The Now 17
Melancholy 18
Shelter 19
Anchor 20
Generosity 21
Separated 22
Detachment 23
Mirror 24
The Night 25
Heart 26
Precaution 27
Elevation 28
Bridge 29
Las Montañas de Bogotá 30
Peaceful Panorama 31
Without Why 32
The Unnameable 33
Recognition 34
Insight 35
Discover 36
The Sense 37

Blind 38
Vanity 39
Visibility 40
To See 41
Unveiling 42
Dream 43
Ajar 44
Mysticism 45

WITNESSES OF A TIME **46**
Net 47
Heaven 48
Metamorphosis 49
The Earthly Paradise 50
Setbacks 51
Alzheimer 52
World Picture 53
Terror 54
Social Media & Co. 55
The Value of Things 56
The Defenseless Word 57
Commemorative Stone 58
The Dead 59
Indoctrinated Intelligence 60
Pollution 61
Indelible? 62
Empathy 63
Blinded 64
Desire 65

Veiled 66
Overcasted 67
Smart Phone 68
Disturbed 69
Freedom 70
Illumination 71
Overshadowed Vision 72
Witnesses of a Time 73
Blinded 74
Artificial Intelligence 75
Useless Prayers 76
Dignified 77
Comfort 78
The Hope 79
Changing 80
Mirage 81

WITHOUT RETURN 82
COVID-19 83
Sign 84
Ephemeral 85
Destiny 86
Without Return 87
Non-Recurring 88
Life and Death 89
Tightrope Walker 90
Whelk Shell 91
Question 92
Autumn 93

Reproduction 94
Migration 95
More 96
Annual Rings 97
What Remains 98
Impotence 99
The Unfathomable 100
Soul 101
Intensity 102
Shadows 103
The Coming and the Going 104
Reversible 105
Ultimate Equality 106
Where To? 107
COVID-19 108
Fugue of Death 109
Borrowed Dawn 110
Lonely Goodbye 111
Final Farewell 112
War in Ukraine 113
Peace Dove 114
Despot 115
Traces 116
Hope 117

About the Author 118
About the Illustrator 122

THE GOAL

The shortest road
is not always the best road
leading to the goal.

MEDITATION

Listen to the silence
until the silence
breaks its silence
and speaks with words
that only the silence knows
how to express.

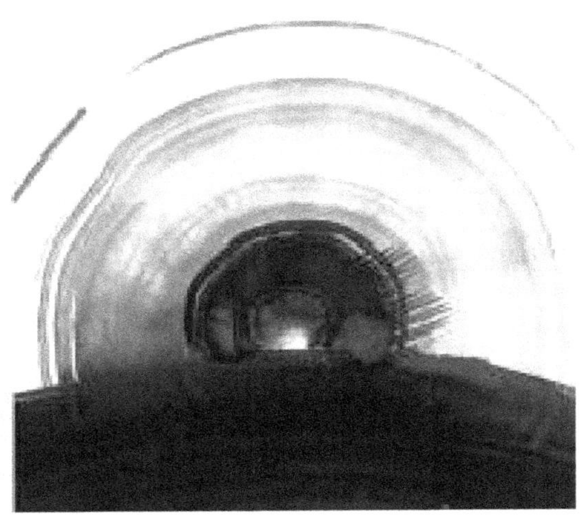

THE LIGHT

It dawns,
the sun rises
out of nowhere

ignites
what only apparently
seems to come from afar

although it is near
and within us:

the light.

Cinders

Although their duration is limited,
the glowing embers spread
what was once fire
warmth and light.

So are also memories
that are not erased—
from better times the cinders,
the enduring glow.

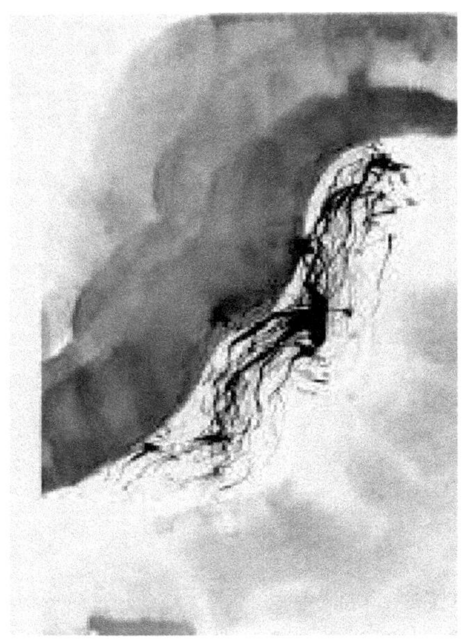

SEARCH

Like the mole,
who digs underground passages,
man don't search for darkness
but for light.

THE NOW

The road to farther
does not always lead to better.

Also the past life
is not always loss
but a road
that sometimes leads inward

to meditation
as well as to values
of the present.

MELANCHOLY

Sometimes it rains softly
barely audible or not at all
as it sometimes rains words
or thoughts
that emerge from a past
that resists
to be bygone.

SHELTER

Not only the house
offers protection and refuge.

Sometimes desire longs
for a shelter of more
than just stone.

ANCHOR

Not every anchor one throws out
offers safety or discovery
of what is deep and unfathomable.

Anchoring is sometimes a standstill
not farther towards more
than what is visible.

Generosity

It is raining
the drops are knocking everywhere
but no one opens.

Only the earth
already months thirsting for water
eagerly receives the heavenly gift

not only for itself.

SEPARATED

An abyss is not an emptiness
but a chasm between two parts
which perhaps once

—not separated

were a unity.

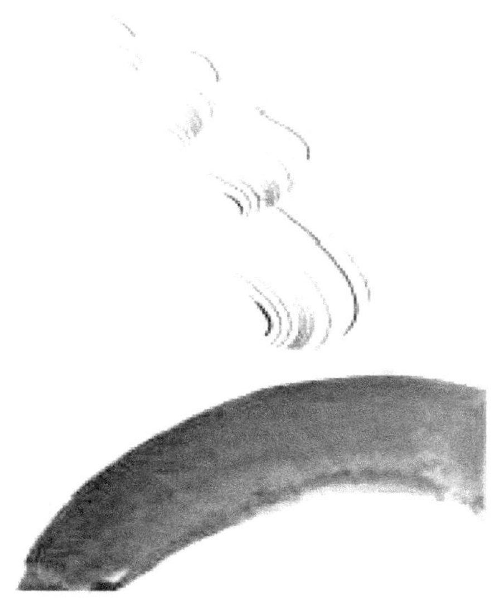

Detachment

But what seeks the bird that flies up
and lifts itself from the earth?

What else does he seeks
than detachment from the things
that are earthly and addictive

—an obstacle

to higher flight.

MIRROR

Memory
is like a mirror
in which one does not see
what one sees
but a reflection
of what one wants to see.

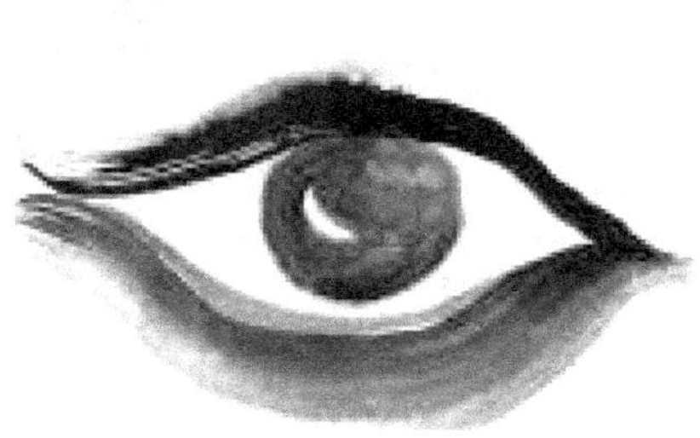

THE NIGHT

Although the night covers
with its darkness the day,
it pleases man's eye
with the display of the moon
and the twinkling light of the stars.

HEART

Do not listen to the heartbeat
as the ticking of a clock
whose duration is finite.

But as a wonder
that can be heard and felt
in the innermost
of one's own being.

PRECAUTION

Keep from speaking
the silver

from silence
the gold

and of happiness
even the crumbs

that can be provisions
for leaner times.

Elevation

The bird that flies up
does not fly
to exalt himself

but to detach itself

—even if only for a moment

from all that is earthly.

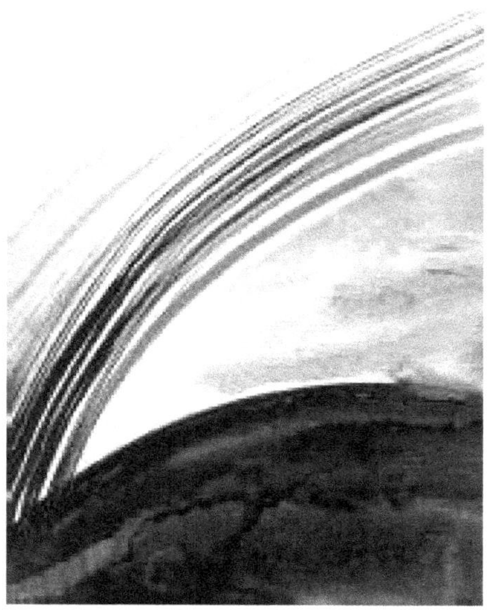

Bridge

A rainbow is more
than a range of colors
that pleases the eye
but a bridge

—that, just for a moment,

connects heaven and earth.

LAS MONTAÑAS DE BOGOTÁ

We greet you from these sunny but sad mountains of Bogotá.

—Eduardo Bechara Navratilova

Cloudless the sky
bathing in sunlight
the mountains
and among the greenery
resounds the sound
of a variety of birds,
the cheerful song

as if prosperity
would not be for some
but for all,
the sky not too high,
happiness not unattainable
and too far away.

Peaceful panorama

Accompanied by birdsong
the dawn appears.

Flowers open
greedily drinking the light
and spreading their perfume.

Over the sharp line of the horizon,
a boat slides over the sea
and the mind
—so turbulent sometimes—
comes for a moment at rest.

Without why

The blossom that opens
and pleases the eye of man
asks no favor in return

selflessly
the blossom gives itself

and dies in beauty
as a flower.

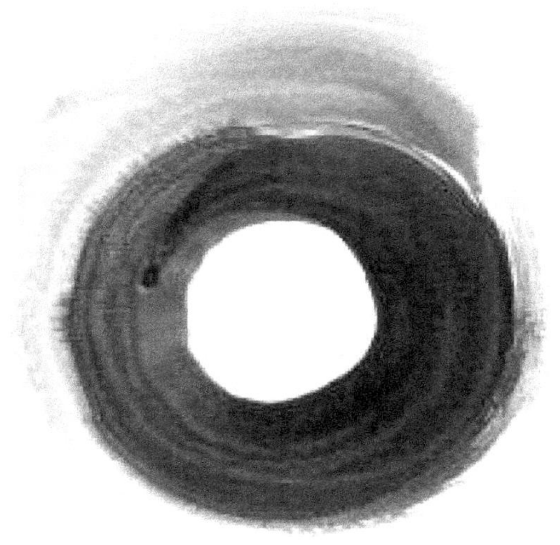

The unnameable

Even if one gives a thousand names
to what is unnameable,
the unnameable
does not reveal its name.

RECOGNITION

Stacked on the writing table, the books
multicolored, large and small, thin and thick
poetry from all over the world.

Peaceful words waiting
for the recognition, for the acceptance
of being distinct and different,
to be allowed to be themselves.

Insight

The creation of a poem
is much more than lines
appearing one by one
on the white sheet.

Poetry is also insight
not only shelter
for the word.

DISCOVER

Writing is not reproducing an existing experience,
but producing one.
—José Ángel Valente

Just as the sunrise does not know
what landscape will appear
when it lights up the earth,
neither does the poet know
what verses will appear
when on the white sheet
the blue ink appears.

Poetry is not the writing of what one knows
but writing what was previously
still unwritten.

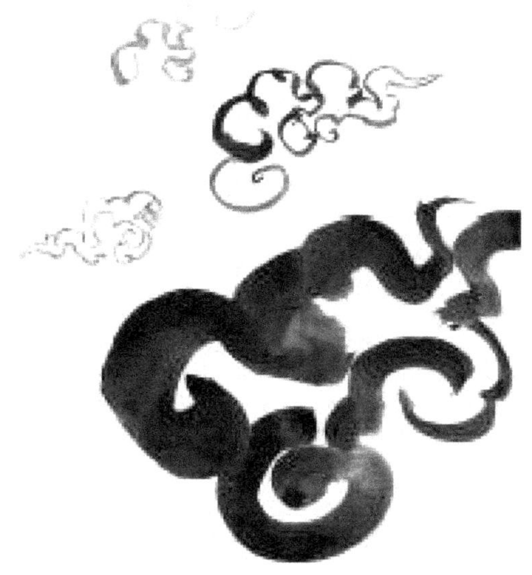

The sense

As white and gray clouds
constantly write their signs
on the blue canvas of the horizon,
the pen writes words
line by line, verses,
on the white sheet.

Sometimes fluently
sometimes hesitating
about the sense of saying.

BLIND

The blind
can neither experience the budding
of the spring blossoms
nor the splendor of colors
of the autumn trees.

But who can see it
and does not see it
is blinder than the blind
who cannot see.

VANITY

What the wind
says to the trees
and what the leaves whisper
will never decipher a human being
who imagines
to know more
than what he knows.

Visibility

As the echo
is only the reverberation of a sound,
so is the mirroring
only the reflection of what is visible,
a reality
which does not reveal everything.

TO SEE

Closing the eyes
does not always result in reduced vision
but sometimes

—directed inwards—

reveals more
than what is seen.

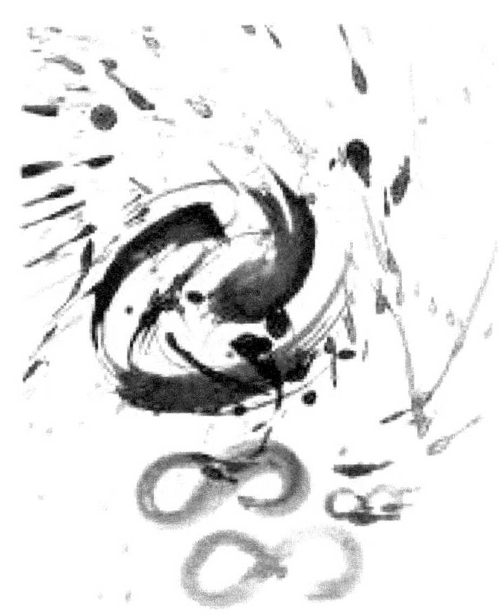

UNVEILING

Sometimes a poem is
a veil

but unveils
what was previously
hidden or veiled.

Dream

Although the dream
is not a reality,
sometimes it shows the way
to a reality
that surpasses the dream.

Ajar

Sometimes a word sets
the darkness ajar
and makes visible
what before was invisible
and lost:
the comfort of hope.

Mysticism

Is there an end
that is not infinite
but a resurrection

an emptiness
that is not emptiness
but fullness?

WITNESSES OF A TIME

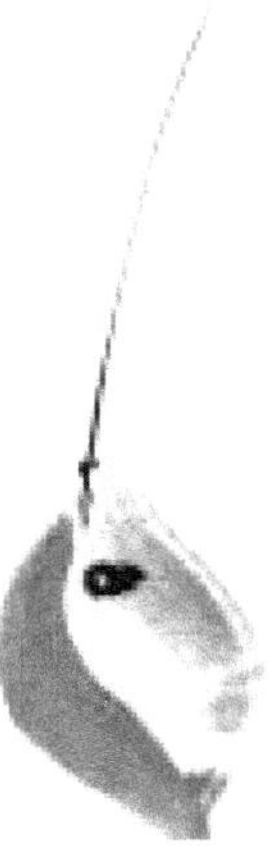

NET

The freedom
of the fish in the sea
is as long freedom
until he is caught.

So are human beings
only free at their birth
not yet caught
in the net.

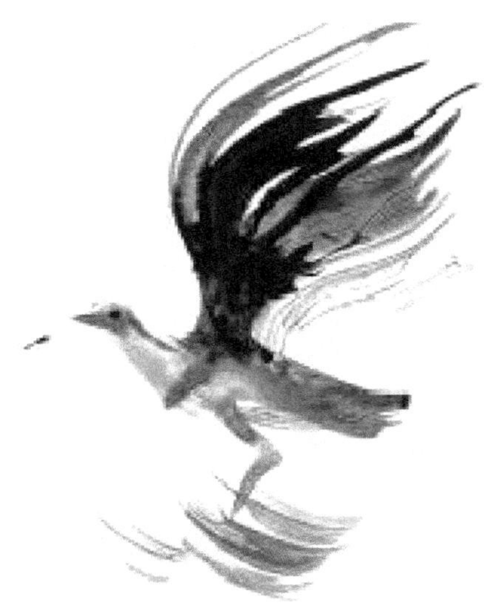

Heaven

It is not heaven
the bird seeks
when it spreads its wings
and flies up.

It knows,
that also for it
heaven is too far
and inscrutable.

METAMORPHOSIS

The serpent was not driven out
from the earthly paradise.

She stayed there all the time

manifolded
and disguised herself
as human.

The earthly paradise

The earthly paradise
has not been lost.

All those centuries
it has continued to exist—
but not for everyone.

SETBACKS

There are setbacks in life, so fierce, I don't know anymore!

—César Vallejo

There are days in life
so homeless and gray
that in their own sadness
they threaten to drown.

Although somewhere

—how or wherever?—

there must be light and shelter
but not always in sight.

ALZHEIMER

Just as the dawn does not suddenly
but gradually arises,
oblivion increases
with the years.

What remains
is the memory of the past
of bygones
which only in memory
know their return.

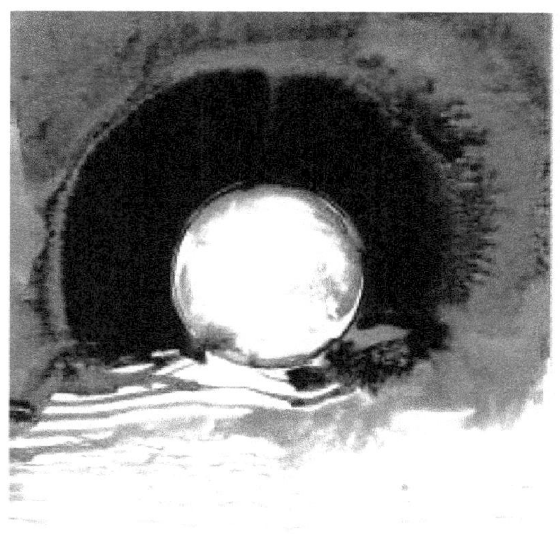

WORLD PICTURE

It dawns . . .
what was darkness before
dissolves without trace into the light

as if elsewhere darkness
and despair do not reign

as if elsewhere were no people
waiting in vain
for light.

Terror

The war is no longer declared but continues.
The unheard has become daily.
—Ingeborg Bachmann

Homes destroyed by missiles
—innocent people, women, children,
killed by the haughty madness
of misleaders.

Unwinged the dove, the truth,
raped by lies.

SOCIAL MEDIA & CO.

Whoever stretches his hand
not only loses his arm
but his identity, too.

THE VALUE OF THINGS

Today, people know the price of everything
and the value of nothing.
—Oscar Wilde

Not all beggars beg for money
although they have a need for things
which not always are available
but are priceless

like a tender word
an embrace
love.

THE DEFENSELESS WORD

How great is the fear of the word
to leave its shelter
naked and defenseless.

And wherever it appears
again and again
mutilated and raped.

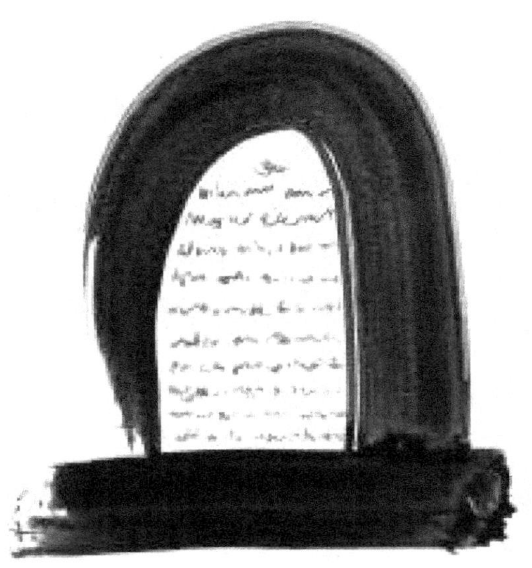

Commemorative stone

Letter after letter
word for word
writes life so long
on its memorial stone
till the stone is full—
and life
is deregistered.

THE DEAD

The dead speak
though one neither hears nor sees them.

They speak with words of silence
which sometimes are more penetrating
than what they ever said before.

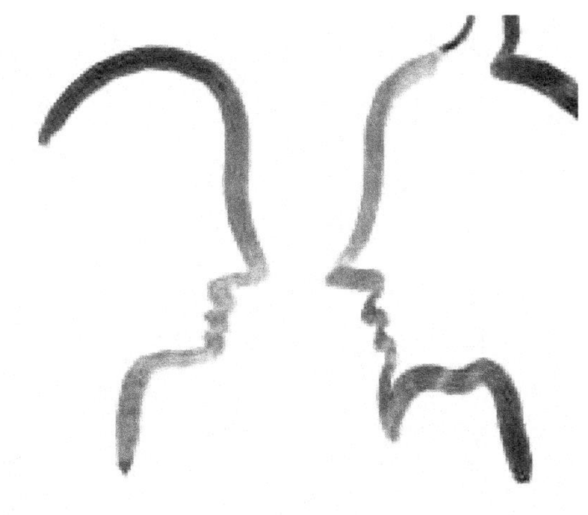

Indoctrinated intelligence

The void
—stripped of all meaning—
has become mundane.

What one should think or do
is preprogrammed.

The image
which we see in the mirror
is no longer our own image.

Pollution

Pollution
covers the earth

contaminates oceans and seas
the rivers and the air
kills birds and fish.

How long
will man survive?

Indelible?

A child
washed ashore by the sea
lies dead on the beach.

Indelible the image.
Or not?

EMPATHY

Even if you lack nothing,
you not only feel your own
but also of the less fortunate . . .
you feel the heartbeat.

Blinded

The night blurs the vision
but does not blind the eye
of human beings.

Neither is it the dawn,
the natural light,
that blinds him.

It is the human being
who blinds more
than merely the eye.

Desire

. . . there is no greater desire
than the desire for fulfillment
—Kurt Tucholsky

Just as the night yearns
for the moon and the stars
and the day for the dawn

so yearn also humans
for more than what memory
has left behind.

VEILED

Sometimes obscured or veiled,
sometimes light in the darkness,
is the moon at night.

She briefly heals the eye
wounded by the excess of images
of injustice and harm
by the despair in the gaze
of a ragged child.

Overcasted

There are days
in which darkness
covers and permeates everything.

Happiness that before
used to be generous and abundant
seems unattainable, too far away.

Although one knows
—or hopes—
that never disappears
all the light.

SMART PHONE

In the waiting room
sits a large number of travelers.

With one notable exception,
all of them are busy
with a little thing called smart phone
that fascinates them all the time.

With two thumbs at the same time
they write their stories,
meaningful or not they are written,
and sent out into the world.

Only one person does not write, but reads,
he reads a book.
Doesn’t he have anything to say?

DISTURBED

Before the horizon
lies apparently motionless,
the blue of the sea,
and the wind gives no sigh.

The poet should now find
the redeeming words,
the verses for a new poem.

But disturbed by noisy voices,
the pen falters,
and the poem remains unwritten.

FREEDOM

The banks of the river
are no restriction
for the river
but show the water
that sometimes is unbridled
and too wild
the road.

ILLUMINATION

Not every night
is studded with stars.

And not every day
has a dawn
that with its colors
pleases the eye.

But the artificial light
does not illuminate more
than the near sight.

Overshadowed vision

Not all shadows are visible
though sometimes they obstruct more
than just the sight.

As through the haze obscured,
the horizon continues to exist,
but is no longer visible
to the eye.

Witnesses of a Time

Just as the rain
erases traces left behind,
disappears by a technical problem
or decision of higher powers
what we once entrusted
to floppy, computer, VHS, or CD.

What will soon remain of us, only yellowed
that once was written on paper
by typewriter or pen—
and of those who come after us,
nothing at all?

BLINDED

Unlike man
who irreversibly disrupts
pollutes and destroys,
the dawn light offers
day by day.

But humans,
blinded by selfishness,
doesn't illuminate the dawn.

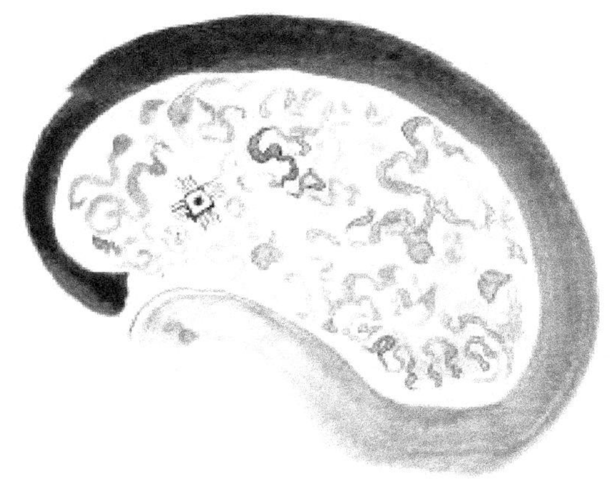

ARTIFICIAL INTELLIGENCE

Rivers overflow their banks
houses are demolished
cars swept away
by the raging waters:
man has disrupted nature.

In vain
wisdom's warning words.

Would a chip, implanted in the brain,
offer more wisdom or even more blindness
and indoctrination?

USELESS PRAYERS

So many calamities take place on earth
continually and increasingly plagued
by disasters and injustice,
although millions of prayers
are daily sent to heaven.

But which God, who speaks all those languages,
can give them a hearing, when it is man
who disrupts even the heavenly vault?

DIGNIFIED

For a bird
that cannot fly anymore
life is no more life.

But is life
that is no longer dignified
still life?

Comfort

Not only the body
that wants to be quenched
needs
food and drink.

Also the dream
which otherwise withers away,
desires a shelter.

THE HOPE

A sheet is like hope
covering what sometimes seems hopeless.

But there are days
—so dull—
that not even the night
equals their darkness.

Although one knows
—or expects—
that after the rain,
the sun will shine.

CHANGING

Everything that is earthly is changeable
but not so far the fate of the human being
who is born
and dies.

But if all earthly is changeable,
how much longer, not man?

MIRAGE

With its broad wing beat
moves a bird the air
which before seemed unmoved
and motionless

as if the sky and the air
would not be changed.

WITHOUT RETURN

COVID-19

It's raining . . .
as if at the sight
of so much sadness
even the sky weeps.

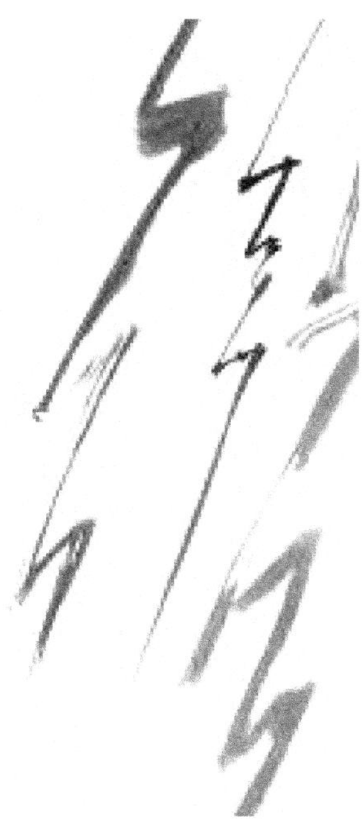

Sign

What else is the lightning
which illuminates the sky for just a moment
than a sign to man
that everything earthly
is ephemeral and transient?

Ephemeral

Although the day flower
lives no more than a day, she doesn't mourn,
but she gives her beauty

—even if it lasts but one day,

her whole life.

DESTINY

Between heaven and earth
constantly changing
until they disappear,
the clouds.

The clouds are like man
who from his birth
constantly changing
comes and goes.

Without return

The branches of the trees
turning yellow in autumn
become green again in spring,

and there is no night
that knows no dawn,

but the passing away
of man
knows neither spring nor return.

NON-RECURRING

Life is like a book
that word for word
but never again
is read
and from which no human
but life itself
turns the pages.

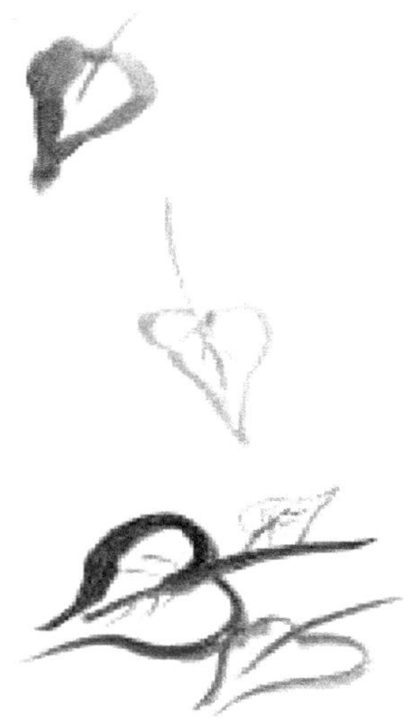

LIFE AND DEATH

Exuberantly celebrates spring
with blossom and flower
its annual revival.

But the old,
the yellowed leaves,
fall compulsively down—

They mingle with the earth—
for them there is neither joy
nor return.

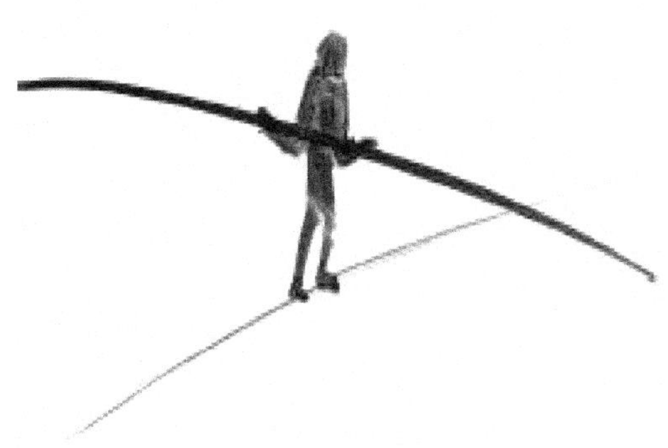

TIGHTROPE WALKER

Equal to an acrobat are human beings
which on the tightrope of life try
to find the sometimes unsteady balance
avoiding the fall that injures
or leads to death.

Whelk shell

The rustling in the whelk shell
is not the beating of the waves
but of time, the fading away
that knows no detention.

QUESTION

Which song
that no one else sings
sings between the branches
of the trees, the wind?

It comes up from nothingness
and into nothingness disappears,
like humans.

Autumn

The leaves die off,
but they do not grieve.

Multicolored adorned
they leave their tree
in a last dance.

Reproduction

When autumn comes
the ripe fruit leaves the tree
intermingles with the earth
out of which in spring
the tree's offspring,
its new life will appear.

MIGRATION

The migration of birds
leads to the warmer,
to their familiar regions.

A long
or short migratory journey
is like human life.

But neither the day
nor the destiny is known.

More

Withered leaves
are more than died-off green
but fertility
for the earth.

So are also deceased more
than died-off life
entrusted to the earth.

Annual rings

Not like human beings
celebrating their aging
counts inwardly the tree,
the passing of years
but celebrates each spring
the return of blossoms and leaves
the resurrection, new life.

WHAT REMAINS

The water wheel
doesn't count
the drops of the stream.

Just as life neither counts
the hours of a human's life

Only the time clock
counts down the days,
the remaining time.

IMPOTENCE

Morning after morning
he goes to the beach

With the songs of the birds
and the blooms of the flowers
he shares the joy, the meaning of life.

But in the insistence of the waves,
he experiences futility,
the fruitless resistance,
against the passage of time.

THE UNFATHOMABLE

The unfathomable
is not only what exists
beyond recognition.

Unfathomable
is also one's own being
and the soul,

and whether it exists
or whatever it is.

Soul

What is invisible
to the eye may exist

but not everything
that is invisible
is one also sure
that it exists.

INTENSITY

It is not the length of time
that makes love
or suffering
greater

but the intensity

the height
or the depth
that remained.

Shadows

Of some days
the shadows are so long
that the light seems too far
or not present.

Although one knows
that there is no shadow
without light.

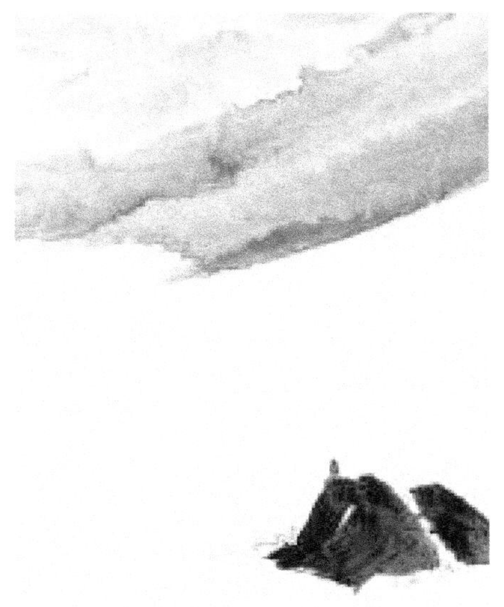

THE COMING AND THE GOING

In the insistence of the waves
crashing against the cliffs
and in the appearance
and disappearance
of the wind he experiences
the limitation of life—
the coming and the going.

Reversible

The irreversible
is the step we have not taken
—Hugo Mujica

Pushing the boundaries
beyond the perceptive.

Turning the irreversible into reversible
when the road to farther
no more offers a farther.

ULTIMATE EQUALITY

How high ever the flight
for rich and poor alike,
life is a path
taking everyone
in the same direction—
to the same end.

Where to?

In the hospital
the dying listens
to the beating
of his own heart
beating irregularly
slower and slower.

He knows the road
wonders
where to?

COVID-19

Greater still
than the solitude of the moon
who sees the stars in plain sight
but can never embrace them
is also the waiting,
the loneliness of man,
who expects of life
nothing more
than the night that knows no dawn.

FUGUE OF DEATH*
(Coronavirus)

Death, we drink you,
we drink you with our eyes,
we drink you with our ears
we drink you day by day.

Dead, no time is left to say goodbye,
no time to dig your graves,
the leaders paved the road
with hypocrisy and dazzling lies.

Death, we drink you,
we drink you with our eyes,
we drink you with our ears
we drink you day by day.

***Todesfuge (**Fugue of Death), famous poem by Paul Celan about the extermination of Jews by the Nazis

Borrowed dawn

With its hand of shadow and darkness,
the defenseless light
unravels the evening

unravels the future
the magic—
the borrowed dawn

pulls out the wick
sheds the oil
extinguishes time.

Lonely goodbye

for those who, wherever, have to die lonely

Chilly the room
the white walls.

Audible only
the echo of loneliness.

Not a tender word anymore,
no warm embrace.

Just the time,
a leaking tap,
ticking.

None knocking at the door
nobody you expect,
no one, except death.

FINAL FAREWELL

Suddenly, whether expected or not,
but unwanted,
there it is
the farewell
that knows no reunion
the very life
that disappears from the body.

Farewell longing
farewell lover
a last embrace
a last kiss
a last look
farewell . . .

War in Ukraine

The almond trees are here in bloom
a delight to the eye
that loves beauty.

Soon the citrus blossoms
will spread their seductive perfume.

But elsewhere rages the war,
the destruction and human suffering.

No blossoms bloom there—
they suffocate in the smoke
of barbarous violence.

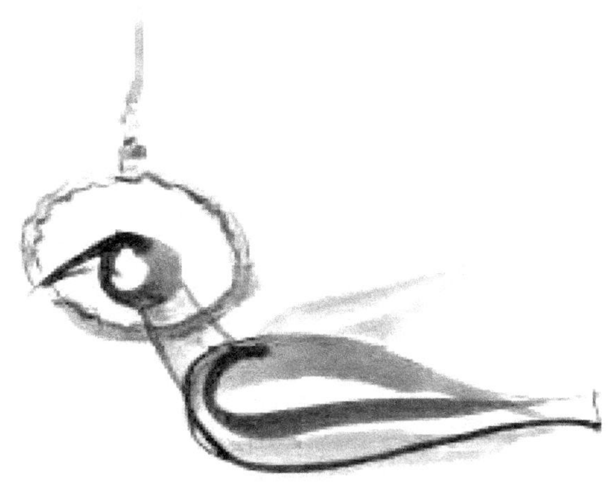

PEACE DOVE

It is raining
it rains sadness

For innocent victims
for the destruction of a country
for the escape of murderous violence.

Hungry, a turtle dove leaves
from the shelter of her tree

Like a noose
the black ring around her neck.

Despot

The night has assaulted the dawn
and steals from peace
the precious light.

Silence dies down
drowned out by gunfire
cannons and howling sirens.

Unmoved by the suffering
—even of his own people—
the power-mad despot.

TRACES

The storm has quieted down:
the grains of sand mingled
with the algae on the beach,
traces of the raging
of violence.

But elsewhere the raging does not stop:
houses are set ablaze
there lie no algae
there lie the dead
like bloody traces
of a murderous war.

Hope

It is winter,
the chilly wind has torn off
the last leaves from the trees
which before were protection
and accommodation for the birds.

They shiver in the cold
but still whistle
because they also hope
for better times.

ABOUT THE AUTHOR

GERMAIN DROOGENBROODT, was born 11 September 1944 in Rollegem, the Flemish part of Belgium. In 1987 he moved to the Mediterranean artist village of Altea and integrated in Spanish literary life.

Germain Droogenbroodt is an internationally appreciated poet, invited yearly at the most prestigious international poetry festivals. He wrote short stories and literary reviews, but mainly poetry, so far sixteen poetry books, published in 30 countries. He is also translator, publisher, and promoter of modern international poetry. He translated – he speaks six languages— more than thirty collections of German, Italian, Spanish, Latin American, English and French poetry, including anthologies of Bertolt Brecht, Mahmud Darwish, Reiner Kunze, Miguel Hernández, José Ángel Valente, Francisco Brines and also rendered Arabic, Chinese, Japanese, Persian and Korean poetry into Dutch.

As founder and editor of the Belgian publishing house POINT Editions (**PO**etry **INT**ernational) he published more than eighty collections of mainly modern, international poetry. In 1996 he set up a new poetic movement, called *neo-sensacionismo* with the famous Chinese poets Bei Dao and Duo Duo

Germain Droogenbroodt organised and co-organised several international poetry festivals in Spain. He is vice president of the Academy Mihai Eminescu, organizing the International Poetry Festival Mihai Eminescu in Craiova, Romania, co-founder, and advisor of JUNPA (Japan Universal Poets Association), artistic advisor of the Italian movement Poetry & Discovery, general counsel of the Chinese cultural Association Huifeng, International Shanghai and is founding president of the Spanish cultural foundation ITHACA. His poetry has been awarded with more than a dozen international poetry Prizes, the latest for his unpublished poetry book *Poetic Reflections* by the Premio Internacional of Fuente Vaqueros, birthplace of Federico García Lorca, in Spain, 2023

His poetic oeuvre is many-sided. After his début with *FORTY AT THE WALL* (1984), defined as neo-romantic poetry, he published "Do you know the country?" *Meditations at Lake* Como (Italy), a collection of nature poems. In 1995 he was awarded a Hawthornden Fellowship (Scotland) where he wrote *CONVERSATION WITH THE HEREAFTER*,"poems about death, awarded in Belgium with the P.G. Buckinx-Prize and *PALPABLE ABSENCE*, a bilingual (Dutch Spanish) collection of love poems. A critic of the Dutch Information Office for Libraries described his love poems as "virtuoso poetry." At the end of 1998 appeared *BETWEEN THE SILENCE OF YOUR LIPS*, his collected love poems.

During his sojourn at the Palace-Fortress "Neemrana" in Rajasthan, 1998, he completed the poetry cycle *THE ROAD*, (read TAO) a poetic bridge between the East and the West, inspiring the Flemish artist Frans Minnaert and the Indian painter Satish Gupta, who enriched *The Road* with their drawings. This philosophical, mystical poetry is so far his most popular book, published already in 25 countries, according to the Icelandic poet-critic Thór Stefansson prophetic, philosophic poetry, translated by such famous poets as Bei Dao (Chinese), Fuad Rifka (Arabic), Jana Stroblova and Josef Hruby (Czech), Milan Richter (Slovak), Emilio Coco, Luca Benassi and Tiziana Orrù (Italian), Ganga Prasad Vimal (Hindi)...

In 2001 he wrote in Spanish *AMANECE EL CANTOR* (*The Singer Awakes*), a homage to the deceased poet José Ángel Valente, followed by *COUNTERLIGHT* written in Ronda (Southern Spain) in 2002, published in Spain by Calima Ediciones, in Romania by ex-Ponto, in Belgium by POINT Editions, in both Mongolian languages by GCompress Co., Ltd. Ulaanbaatar, in Arab by

Albayat (Morocco), in Hong Kong by "Contemporary Poetry," and in Taiwan by Poet Culture. Corp. The latter publication includes also *COUNTER LIGHT*.

His poetry book *IN THE STREAM OF TIME, Meditations in the Himalayas,* was published in 2008 in Belgium and as part of *Selected Poems by Germain Droogenbroodt*, 2008 in Shanghai by the Shanghai Literature & Art Publishing Group and in Spain, laureate of the *XXIX Premio de Poesía Juan Alcaide 2008*. Struga Poetry Evenings also published *IN THE STREAM OF TIME* in their prestigious *Pleiades* in 2010. The book was also translated in Japanese and launched at the Kyoto City International Foundation in Kyoto, Japan in 2010 and in Gaelic (Irish) in 2012. A selection of his poems was also published in Bengal in Bangladesh (2012 and 2015). *UNSHADOWED LIGHT*, was launched end 2012 in a bilingual Dutch-Spanish publication at the Book Fair in Antwerp and in several Belgian towns and in Spain. *IN THE STREAM OF TIME, Meditations in the Himalayas*" was published in Romania in 2015.

The anthology *THE DEWDROPS OF DAWN*, a selection from 11 poetry books, was published with illustrations by Satish Gupta in German, in Dutch and in Croatian (2014). *DEWDROPS*, a selection of 100 haiku in Japanese, English, Spanish, and Dutch was published by JUNPA, Kyoto, and launched in Japan end 2016. His last but one poetry book, *THE EPHEMERAL FLOWER OF TIME* was published end 2016 in Dutch and Spanish and in English (2017) and in 2021 in Serbia, in Japan and in China. *THE ORACLE OF TIME*, published 2019 in the US. His last but one book *The Unrest of the Word* was published Dutch-Spanish in Belgium and Holland and Dancing Butterfly, his second collection of haiku, as published end 2022 in Japan. *THE ROAD OF BEING*, his latest poetry book, has already been published in 2023 in Belgium, Bangladesh, Chile, Holland, and Pakistan.

Several famous artists made paintings and sculptures inspired by his poetry as international composers composed music to poems, such as the Dutch composer Bart Bakker who composed the *Germain Droogenbroodt cycle,* 12 pieces for flute.

Germain Droogenbroodt is yearly invited to give recitals and conferences at universities and at the most prestigious poetry festivals around the world. He was recommended for the Nobel Prize of Literature 2017.

About the Artist

SATISH GUPTA is India's celebrated painter, sculptor, poet, writer, printmaker, skilled draftsman, muralist, designer, and calligrapher all in one. His works have a deep engagement with mysticism and Zen spirit. Drawing inspiration from the roots of Indian civilization and its rich cultural storehouse, he brings a spirit of positivity and hope to his works and finds his inspiration from an inner peace and tranquility that is a benchmark of his works. His paintings and sculptures are in museums worldwide, including in Shanghai Museum of Modern Art, The Museum of Sacred Arts, Brussels, and The National Museum in Slovenia. He had over 40 solo shows in reputed galleries in Houston, New York, Washington, San Francisco, Vancouver, Ottawa, London, Paris, Murcia, Altea, Sylt, Moscow, Singapore, Melbourne, Delhi, Kolkata, Mumbai, and Chennai.

Satish Gupta is also known for his monumental copper sculptures: The 23-foot-wide sculpture, *The Buddhas Within*, is in the permanent collection of The Prince of Wales Museum (CMVS) in Mumbai. He also created a 11-foot-high sculpture of the Sun god, Surya, at the T3 at Delhi airport; the Devi at The Leela palace hotel in Chanakyapuri, New Delhi; Zen Forest in Ritz Carlton in Bangalore; and a 33 foot mural at the International Airport called *The Lotus Sutra* in the same city. *Meditations on a Mandala*, his sculpture in copper was displayed at Art Laguna Prize, Arsenal and at the India Art Fair 2023.

His book, *Zen Whispers*, was released at the Jaipur Literature Festival in 2018 and he read his poems in many poetry festivals, they were published in Spanish and in Catalan. He created a one-mile-long calligraphic canvas, *MA*, to bring awareness about global warming along the beach in Pondicherry. This is perhaps the longest canvas in the world. *Roaring Sea – Still Mind*, an exhibition of his large sculptures, paintings, and calligraphic works was displayed at The Visual Arts Gallery at The Indian Habitat Centre, Delhi in 2019. This exhibition was also displayed in Los Angeles and at Gallery Falkenstern Fine Art in Germany. He lives in New Delhi with his designer wife Amita and paints in his Zen studio in Gurgaon on the outskirts of Delhi.

www.ingramcontent.com/pod-product-compliance
Lightning Source LLC
LaVergne TN
LVHW010933110826
845149LV00013B/2582

* 9 7 8 1 9 6 0 0 3 8 3 5 7 *